I0427827

Puppy Training Guide:

A Proven and Powerful Guide to Training Your Puppy in Obedience, Potty Training and Much More

Table of Contents

Introduction

I want to thank you and congratulate you for downloading the book *Puppy Training Guide: A Proven and Powerful Guide to Training Your Puppy in Obedience, Potty Training and Much More.*

This book contains proven steps and strategies on how to become a truly terrific puppy trainer. We'll have you turning your puppy from a rambunctious, unruly ball of fur into a model canine citizen in no time!

Here's an inescapable fact: Puppy training is not an easy job. You will need to train your puppy not to pee all over your carpet. And not to bark at innocent passersby. And not to chew your curtains to bits. And to listen and obey your commands. Puppy training is a *lot* of work.

Unfortunately, puppies don't come with any factory settings that tell them to be well-behaved. You have to do it yourself! This book will provide all the information you need to train your new dog and will explain the steps to becoming a successful puppy trainer in a clear and easy-to-understand manner.

If you do not develop your puppy training skills, you'll quickly find yourself stuck with a fully grown, misbehaving dog that refuses to listen to you, ruins your home, and is rude to your family and guests. Once a dog has developed negative habits, it can be challenging to change them. It's important to start teaching your puppy to behave correctly from the beginning so that you can avoid all the heartache, annoyance, and stained carpets that are sure to accompany a poorly trained dog.

Are you ready to learn everything there is to know about working with puppies? It's time for you to become a puppy trainer extraordinaire!

Chapter 1: Puppy Training Basics

There are few things more exciting than bringing home a brand new puppy. Perhaps you've been searching for months, trying to find *the one*, or maybe you simply stumbled across an abandoned stray at the side of the road and realized that yours could be the family to give him a warm, safe, and happy home. Either way, you now have a new member of your family, and your household is sure to be brimming with excitement, eager to get off on the right foot.

While puppies can be messy, smelly, destructive, and rambunctious, they can also be loving, loyal, warm, and buckets of fun! While you need to be prepared to deal with the trouble and chaos that a puppy can bring to your house, you can minimize the collateral damage by treating your puppy the right way from the minute he joins your family.

To ensure that your puppy will be on his best behavior and will become a welcome and beloved addition to your household, it's important to get started with training right away. After all, puppies start developing habits and behavior that will follow them into adulthood from the moment you bring them home. It's much easier for a puppy to learn proper behavior the first time around than to unlearn bad habits once they're older.

Before bringing a puppy home, make sure that you and your family know the basic guidelines of dog training.

The Importance of Consistency and Mannerisms

For starters, it's essential to understand the importance of consistency. If your behavior, rules, and commands change day by day, your puppy will quickly become confused and unable to understand what you expect from him. Instead, establish rules that nobody will bend, no matter how persuasive your puppy's "puppy dog eyes."

Once everyone understands the expectations for your new puppy's behavior, you need to know how to implement these rules. Dogs are extremely perceptive, and so it's important to know how to address them and to encourage them to behave a certain way.

Always remain calm when speaking to your puppy. Although he may do something that you want to discourage, such as relieving himself on the carpet, don't punish your puppy – and certainly, never use physical punishment to try to teach your puppy a lesson. A punishment even as seemingly harmless as a thorough scolding can cause your puppy to form a negative association with a natural situation and to feel confused, upset, and unloved.

Instead of punishing your puppy for bad behavior, show them an alternative, desired behavior and provide appropriate rewards.

This, too, demands consistency. Establish certain rewards to be provided when the puppy demonstrates a positive behavior, and ensure that everyone in your household knows what the reward is and when it should be provided. This will help your puppy understand what is good and what isn't, and it will make it easier for you to monitor how many treats he's eating. After all, you don't want to instill good behavior at the cost of your puppy's health and well-being!

Understanding Dog Breeds and Differences

When learning the basics about how to train your new puppy, it can also help to understand the differences between dog breeds and what this will mean for you. While a dog's individual and unique personality certainly impacts their behavior and their response to training, breed can give you some idea about how your dog is likely to behave.

Some breeds are known for their intelligence and laid-back natures, while others tend to be stubborn and self-indulgent. For example, Afghan Hounds and Dalmatians are famous for being stubborn or easily distracted, but Corgis, Australian Shepherds, and Poodles are generally some of the easiest breeds to train. You may decide that a certain breed is worth the difficulty it may present in training, but it's up to you to choose what your family is looking for in a dog.

If you haven't yet picked out a puppy, it can be helpful to do some preliminary research on the standard dispositions and ease of training for various dog breeds. Some families have the time and space necessary for more high-maintenance dogs, while others might find themselves opting for obedient breeds that are easier to train. It's up to you to decide what you're looking for in a dog and to prepare accordingly.

If you've already found your puppy, however, you can still do research to learn more about what to expect as you train him. For a dog whose breed tends to create difficulties in training, it may be helpful to prepare yourself for any frustrations that come along the way. No matter how easy or challenging it is to train a puppy, it's important that you're able to control your emotions and remain calm and consistent.

Caring for Your Puppy

Before you dive into training, you also need to know how to take care of your dog. If your puppy is healthy, comfortable, and placed in an ideal environment for optimal learning, you'll likely find training easier than if your puppy weren't content.

Make sure you have all the supplies you need for raising a puppy: a bed or crate of some sort, a brush, food and water, toys, treats, a collar with tags, and a leash. Select items that are well-suited for your new puppy, sure to fit properly and ensure his comfort.

Also, remember that your puppy isn't the only one who needs to begin developing good habits early on! You should know how to take care of him properly from the day you bring him home. For example, you should avoid free feeding, or leaving your dog's food out at all hours of the day. Instead, develop a regular feeding schedule and provide the proper amount of food only at certain hours of the day. Not only is this better for your dog's health, as it prevents overeating, but it also helps him to view you as his "pack leader," the one responsible for providing food. This association will help him to develop a healthy level of respect for you and any other providers, and this will make training all the easier.

Once you've got your pup settled in with all his new belongings and routines, you should schedule an appointment with a veterinarian as soon as you can. Make sure your puppy has all the vaccinations he needs (see Chapter 5) and is in good health; in some instances, a health condition can cause behavioral issues, so it's beneficial to rule out any sort of illness before you begin training.

Your vet may also provide useful information about caring for a puppy. Veterinarians are often knowledgeable about various dog breeds and stages of development, and they can provide tips that help you become a better caregiver.

Once your puppy is healthy and well provided for, you're ready to begin! You'll have your dog properly trained in no time.

Chapter 2: Behavior Training

One of the most important parts of dog training is behavior training; after all, a misbehaving puppy can often be an expensive nuisance. No one wants to be woken up at 2 a.m. by a dog that won't stop barking, or to have to replace all the furniture in the house because your puppy won't stop chewing on everything.

There are many different aspects of behavior training, and each has its own steps and techniques. However, the general idea is to use the tips discussed in the previous chapter: reward your puppy for desired behaviors and maintain a consistent training routine.

Potty Training

There is nothing worse than getting out of bed and setting your feet on the floor, only to discover that your puppy left you a lovely, squishy, smelly surprise overnight. While this disgusting and, frankly, borderline traumatizing experience can be avoided by confining your puppy to a crate or other designated sleeping area and keeping a close eye on him during the day, you can circumvent the entire issue by starting to potty train your puppy right away.

A puppy is never too young to begin learning where to use the bathroom and, perhaps more importantly, where *not* to. However, you should understand that young puppies don't have complete control over their bladders and bowels. Even once they learn that they shouldn't pee on your carpet, accidents may still happen simply because they can't control their digestive system.

This makes it even more important that you remain patient with your puppy and never lose your temper; you don't want your puppy to associate negative emotions with a natural process such as going to the restroom. Otherwise, they may begin hiding accidents from you, and instead of training your puppy to go to the bathroom outside, you will have trained him to pee under the table, or poop in a remote corner.

So, how do you avoid accidents from the beginning? The first step is to always keep a watchful eye on your pup. Puppies are so small that they have to go to the bathroom regularly. It's not unusual for a young puppy to have to eliminate every half hour, so you need to provide regular potty breaks. First thing in the morning, right after eating or drinking, right before bedtime, and at regular, 45-minute intervals, you should escort your puppy to his designated potty location – usually a particular spot outdoors, unless you're potty training your puppy using a bathroom or pen inside. Also, you should always use the same door to access your puppy's toilet area, as this will help him associate that door with going to the bathroom, and your puppy will be better able to indicate to you that he needs to go outside.

When you take your puppy to the designated location, use a consistent command such as "go potty" and wait for him to attend to his business. Whenever your puppy eliminates in his designated toilet area, reward him with a treat and/or verbal praises. After some time, your puppy should come to positively associate this location with using the bathroom, and he will naturally want to go to it whenever he needs to relieve himself.

However, until that point, it's essential that you watch closely over your puppy at all times. If you catch him starting to pee or poop anywhere other than his potty location, quickly grab him and move to the correct place if you can. The goal is to startle your puppy enough to stop him until he can resume in his toilet area. However, you should note that puppies often have much more difficulty stopping in the middle of pooping than peeing, and you run the risk of creating a big mess if you try to move them once they've started to poop. It may be better to let your puppy finish where he is before showing him the correct spot.

Never scold or punish your puppy for accidents, and instead focus on rewarding him for correct behavior.

If you're too late to stop your puppy and he has already gone on your floor, you have to clean up the mess thoroughly. Dogs have a highly developed sense of smell, and your puppy will likely return to the same spot if he can still smell the residue of his urine.

You also need to be careful with certain cleaners. Your puppy may mistake the ammonia in a number of common household cleaning products for another dog's urine, and he may pee in the same location to cover up the smell. Instead, look for products that are specially designed to clean up pet messes, as they completely remove the odor, rather than simply covering it up to human senses.

You can gradually increase the time between potty breaks as your puppy develops better control over his bladder and bowels and learns where you want him to go to the bathroom. Once your puppy is three months old, he ought to be reasonably well housetrained, although mistakes may still happen, and by four months, he may be able to "hold it" for up to four hours. However, you still want to be careful to avoid accidents.

Ideally, your puppy will naturally begin to indicate when he needs to go to the bathroom, such as by whining to get your attention or waiting by the door. Your puppy will likely choose some way to tell you to let him outside all by himself, but some people choose to train their dog to alert them that he needs to use the bathroom. For example, one popular choice is to teach your dog to ring a bell whenever he wants to be let outside. This can be accomplished easily enough by installing a bell near the door and ringing it each time you take your pup outside. Soon enough, he should catch on and will ring the door when he wants to be let out.

You may also choose to have a puppy door installed if you have a safe, fenced-in backyard area where your puppy can go to the bathroom. This way, he can have round-the-clock access to his potty location and won't need you to let him outside every time he has to go. You can train your puppy to use a pet door by raising the flap and baiting him from the other side, rewarding him when he comes through, and then gradually encouraging him to push his way through when the flap is down. Most dogs are able to learn how to use a pet door with little trouble.

Once your puppy is telling you when he has to use the bathroom and mostly going in his designated spot, he's potty trained! You may notice some regressions, particularly accompanying sexual maturity, but you and your puppy will get through them with patience and positive encouragement. Congratulations! You've done it.

<u>Training Your Puppy to Use a Leash</u>

Most puppies absolutely love going on walks; it's an opportunity for them to stretch their legs, get some fresh air, and trek through the vast outdoors. Your neighborhood alone is like a great, foreign world, full of curious sights and sounds that your puppy will be eager to explore.

However, walking your pup isn't quite as simple as putting on their leash and stepping outside. Untrained dogs often pull against their leashes, eager to chase after wildlife or stop and smell every single plant they pass by. This is not only a nuisance for you but can also cause long-term health problems for your dog.

You'll want to train your puppy to walk politely, which includes learning not to tug on the leash and not to switch sides, entangling you in the leash. Instead, your puppy should walk steadily on one side of you, obeying your commands and following where you lead.

To start with, make sure your puppy has a well-fitted collar and a leash of the appropriate length. You may also consider investing in a harness, which can reduce any negative health effects that result from tugging on the leash. Make sure you also come prepared with treats to reward your puppy for good behavior on the walk.

Once you start walking, reward your puppy every time he walks without pulling and allows the leash to go somewhat slack. While this may be challenging with wilder dogs, there will come a time when even the most high-spirited puppy pauses for a moment and relaxes against the leash. Offer him a treat whenever he does.

When your puppy pulls against the leash, stop moving entirely. Puppies pull because they're eager to move forward, so teaching them that pulling slows rather than hastens progress can help them drop the habit.

By rewarding your puppy when he doesn't pull on the leash and not reacting when he does, he will soon learn to walk politely, without trying to tug you forward.

Next, you can train your pup to stay on one side of you as you walk, instead of weaving back and forth until you're struggling not to trip on the leash. To start with, hold the leash so it's short enough to keep your puppy by your side, but don't pull it so short that you're dragging him along. Reward your puppy regularly when he stays in the correct area, increasing the amount of time between rewards as he realizes what you want from him.

And voila! Your puppy will be walking obediently at your side in no time.

Puppy Manners

In addition to potty and leash training, it's also important to teach your puppy to have good manners. Nobody wants a dog that jumps up on people, begs for table scraps, chews on or scratches furniture, and barks at everything that moves.

The key to teaching your puppy manners is to ignore bad behavior. Many of a puppy's bad habits are designed to get attention or treats, and so teaching your puppy that they won't work is essential to stopping the behavior in its tracks. As in all aspects of puppy training, you must be consistent; indulging your puppy only a few times will reinforce his bad habits.

If your puppy jumps up on people when he's excited, ignore him until all his feet are on the floor. Then, reward him with praise and attention. After some time, your puppy should receive the message that jumping for attention doesn't work.

A similar strategy solves the problem of a dog that begs for snacks while you're trying to eat dinner. As difficult as it may be to ignore your puppy's adorable eyes and pathetic whining, never give food to a begging dog. Doing so only reinforces the idea that begging is an effective way to get treats. Instead, completely ignore your puppy when he begs and refuse to acknowledge him in any way.

Like babies, puppies go through a stage when they like to chew on anything and everything. While this is important for the development of their teeth, it's less than ideal for your furniture. In order to keep your puppy from wreaking havoc in your home, keep a close eye on him at all times. Provide toys for your puppy to chew on. If he attempts to bite anything he shouldn't, offer him the toy instead, and reward him when he starts to play with it. You may reprimand your puppy when you catch him biting something he shouldn't, but the focus should always be on rewarding him for positive behavior instead of scolding negative behavior. If this doesn't seem to work, you can also purchase bitter sprays. The unpleasant taste will dissuade your puppy from chewing on things he shouldn't.

If the problem isn't that your puppy is chewing on your furniture, but that he's chewing on *you*, another technique might work. Puppies generally learn to control biting through playing with other animals, and so you can teach him not to bite too hard through play. When you're playing with your puppy, allow him to bite you, but if he bites too hard, yelp loudly. This should startle your puppy, and ideally he will realize that he has hurt you and will become gentler or will lick you instead. Reward him whenever he does so. As you continue to demonstrate pain whenever your puppy bites too hard, he will learn to control his natural instinct to bite.

Barking is another natural habit that puppies need to be taught to control. While barking can prove beneficial, such as by warning you of unwanted visitors, you don't want your puppy to bark 24/7, whenever someone walks in front of your house or knocks on your door. To train your puppy not to bark all the time, ignore him when he barks for attention and instead reward him for being quiet or seeking your attention in other ways. Obedience training can also be beneficial, as you can teach your dog to "speak," which will grant you some control over the noise he makes.

You can apply these same principles to any other bad habit that your puppy demonstrates, and pretty soon, you'll have a prim and proper puppy!

Chapter 3: Obedience Training

Obedience training is not only an enjoyable way to teach your puppy to perform entertaining tricks, but it also improves communication between you and your puppy and establishes you as the "alpha," so to speak, or the leader of the pack. By training your dog to obey your simple commands, you also teach him to respect and obey you as his master.

While the classic adage that an old dog can't learn new tricks is far from true, a dog is also never too young to begin obedience training. You can start teaching your puppy a few simple tricks on the very day you bring him home.

You may want to enroll in a puppy training class at your local pet store so that you and your puppy can learn the basics, but the bulk of your puppy's training must occur in your own home. Your puppy will learn best when he's in an environment that is familiar and comfortable, and you alone will be responsible for the bulk of his training.

When your puppy is particularly young, training sessions should be short and simple. Your puppy does not yet have the attention span to devote to lengthy lessons in obedience. Instead, try to scatter multiple, five-minute sessions throughout the day.

If your puppy doesn't respond to a command at first, avoid repeating the command, hoping that he'll react. If you say the command multiple times before your puppy obeys, he may develop the idea that he must wait for you to repeat the command before he responds.

To make training easier, you should also generally avoid chattering at your puppy for no reason. Some people enjoy talking to their dogs as if they were people, but if your puppy constantly hears a stream of words coming from your mouth, he may begin to tune you out. By speaking to your puppy less frequently, he's more likely to pay close attention to your commands.

While you can find more in-depth information about the steps to training your dog to respond to specific commands either online or in a class, provided below are the basic steps to train your puppy to obey some of the most basic and useful commands.

"Sit"

Sit is one of the most fundamental commands, as it's easy to teach and allows you to have a lot of control over your puppy. To train your puppy to sit, get a treat and hold it in your closed hand slightly above his nose. Say "sit" in a firm but patient voice. As your puppy looks up at the treat, his behind should lower slightly. You can help him along by gently pushing down on his rump until he's in a sitting position. Once he sits, reward him with the treat and verbal praise, such as "nice" or "good puppy."

You can practice this command several times per training session, but your puppy will tire of too much repetition. You don't want to practice the same command so many times that your pup grows bored.

As your puppy become more familiar with the command, you can decrease the frequency with which you reward him. For example, start to reward your puppy only for particularly quick responses to your command. Eventually, he will obey you without the promise of treats. However, you should continue to praise him each time he successfully obeys your command.

"Down"

Once your puppy has mastered "sit," you can move on to another command. "Down" is also quite simple and easy to teach, and so makes a good second lesson.

To teach your puppy to lie down, catch his attention by holding a treat in front of him. Once he's noticed the treat, lower your hand to the ground and say "down." Your pup should follow the treat down, and once he's lying on the ground, you should reward him with the treat and verbal praise

If your puppy's back end rises after he lies down or if he tries to move forward to the treat, don't reward him. Instead, start again and wait until he lies down completely.

Once your puppy has learned the basic command, reward him less frequently until he obeys without the lure of a treat.

"Stay"

While "stay" can be a more difficult command to teach, it can be particularly useful as the "stay" command allows you to keep your puppy from chasing after another dog or running off when someone momentarily forgets to close the front door.

To train your puppy to stay, begin by placing him in one location. It may be helpful to command your puppy to sit before you begin to move away. Once your pup is holding still, raise your hand, palm facing forward, toward him and say "stay." Then take a few slow steps away. If your puppy stays in place, return to his side and reward him with a treat and praise. If he moves, say something like "nope" or "oops" and place him back where he was before repeating the process.

As your puppy becomes familiar with the command, increase the distance you move before rewarding him. Once your puppy has mastered "stay," you should even be able to leave the room while he remains in place.

"Come"

Much like "stay," the "come" command is highly useful in managing your puppy's behavior. If your puppy escapes and runs amok in your neighborhood, you can call him back with "come," or you can simply use it for a quick and easy way to draw your puppy's attention at meal- or bedtimes.

One of the first steps to training your puppy to come is to train him to recognize his name. Make sure to reward your puppy whenever he responds to his name; otherwise, your puppy may begin to tune out his name because he hears it so regularly without receiving any confirmation. If you can successfully get your puppy's attention by saying his name, it will be easier to teach your pup to come when called.

To train your puppy to come, simply call to him and reward him when he runs to you. This is particularly easy with younger puppies, as they naturally remain close to their owners and gravitate towards them for attention. Make sure that when you call your puppy, you remain cheerful, energetic, and encouraging. Reward your puppy with enthusiastic praise as soon as he responds to your command, rather than waiting until he arrives by your side. This will reduce the risk of your puppy becoming distracted and stopping halfway through his response.

Once your puppy has mastered the basic "come" command, begin increasing the distance between you and your puppy when you issue the command and start practicing in more distracting areas. Even if your puppy obeys you in the quiet and comfort of your own home, that doesn't mean he will behave the same in the middle of the street or the park, for example. If you want your puppy to obey you in all situations, it's important that you practice in other places as well.

These four commands are some of the most basic and useful that you can teach your puppy. However, once your pup has mastered these, there are many others that you can teach as well. Everyone loves a dog that can roll over, play dead, or shake hands, after all. With the right attitude and plenty of patience, training can become a fun activity for both you and your puppy, resulting in a closer relationship between the two of you and a generally better-behaved dog.

Chapter 4: Puppy Socialization

Imagine that you shut a human baby up in his bedroom, never to see anyone but his loving parents. While the baby might be taught to feed himself, to play politely, and to obey his parents, he would never be a well-adjusted member of society. In fact, if the child ever stepped out of his house and met a stranger, or saw an airplane, or stumbled across a skyscraper, he might be terrified and react in entirely inappropriate ways, having never learned how to interact with others or to face the rest of the world.

Puppies are no different. Young pups go through an important stage of development in which socialization is essential. To become a healthy, well-behaved dog, your puppy needs to spend time around other people and animals and be exposed to as many different stimuli as possible.

Socialization is most important in puppies under the age of three or four months, as this is the time when they are forming their ideas about what is normal and becoming familiar with the world around them. If you fail to socialize your puppy appropriately during this time, he may grow up to be shy and skittish, even becoming aggressive in unfamiliar situations.

The first thing you have to do when socializing your puppy is prepare an environment that is calm and reassuring. You don't want your puppy to associate socializing with any sort of negative emotion. In fact, a frightening first encounter with others could leave your puppy scarred for life and unable to overcome a phobia of social interaction.

At the same time, you don't want to accidentally reward fearful behavior in an attempt to calm your puppy. Instead of petting your pup or offering treats to keep him calm, simply speak in a soothing voice and let him see that you're still there. Some signs of fear or stress are to be expected, and your puppy will have to work his way through these emotions to become comfortable with others.

Never push your puppy out of his comfort zone, instead allowing him to adapt at his own pace to the new situations that he faces. Reward your puppy for curiosity and bravery, but never scold him for retreating.

You have the most control over introducing your pup to other humans, as it can be difficult to predict the behavior of animals. Start by inviting your friends and neighbors over to meet your new puppy, and remind them to be calm and gentle. You'll both need to be patient, as your puppy may be fearful and hesitant at first until he becomes used to the new presence.

You'll also want to ensure that your puppy meets a variety of individuals. A pup that never meets a teenaged boy or a black woman, for example, could remain frightened of individuals that meet that profile for the rest of his life. Try to invite people of every ethnicity, age, and gender over to meet your puppy.

Once your puppy has become accustomed to the company of other people, try introducing him to some different animals. Find out if any of your friends have sociable (as well as healthy and vaccinated!) pets that could come over to meet your puppy. If your puppy seems particularly adventurous, you could even take him over to someone else's house to meet their pets, but always remain cautious to ensure your puppy's comfort and safety.

You may have to ease your puppy into interactions with others, such as by holding him yourself until he becomes more comfortable in their presence. Just remember to always be patient and keep a positive attitude.

It may be best to keep such social engagements brief. Although puppies often seem like bouncing balls of energy, they tire quickly, and new, potentially stressful situations can be particularly exhausting for your pup. Try to have brief but frequent socialization periods, rather than a few lengthy engagements.

Apart from individual introductions, you can also take your puppy on short trips to public areas that are full of people or animals. Being surrounded by all the movement and noise can help your puppy become more comfortable with crowds and busy environments.

Introducing your puppy to various locations is also beneficial. Take him for car trips, on a visit to the vet's office, and on a playdate to the park. Allow him to explore these areas, feeling, smelling, and seeing all the different things he can find. Expose your puppy to all sorts of regular experiences, such as hearing police sirens, riding in an elevator, and sitting through a thunderstorm. This will help your puppy to avoid developing phobias to any of these things as he grows older.

Once your puppy has encountered all sorts of different people, pets, and environments, you'll have a much more good-tempered and well-adjusted dog. Plus, he (and you!) may even make some friends along the way.

Chapter 5: Puppy Vaccinations

There's no point to having an obedient, well-trained puppy if he's also unhealthy and sick.

It takes a lot of effort to keep a puppy healthy. After all, puppies get into a lot of things they shouldn't. Whether your pup's digging in the garden, rifling through your trash, or playing with the neighborhood stray, he could be exposing himself to all sorts of germs and diseases.

Luckily, veterinarians can provide a number of vaccinations that your puppy needs during the first year. While you'll need to keep your puppy up-to-date on vaccinations throughout the entirety of his life, this first year is the most important time to ensure the health of your pup.

Even if you've bought a puppy who has already received the first round of vaccines, schedule an appointment with your veterinarian as soon as you can upon picking out your new puppy. Your veterinarian can provide more information about which vaccines your puppy needs and when, as well as a general check-up to make sure your pup doesn't have any diseases that need treatment.

While your vet can provide more detailed information tailored to your puppy in particular, here is the general schedule of puppy vaccinations:

1. 6-8 weeks: Your puppy should be vaccinated against distemper, hepatitis, parvovirus, and parainfluenza. This is usually done in a combination vaccine called DHPP. He may also receive a vaccine for bordatella.

2. 10-12 weeks: Your pup will receive the second round of DHPP. Your puppy's breed and other risk factors will determine whether he also gets vaccines for diseases such as coronavirus, Lyme disease, kennel cough, and leptospirosis.

3. 12-24 weeks: During this time period, your puppy should receive the third and fourth injections of DHPP, as well as two injections of a rabies vaccine. Your veterinarian may also decide to administer other vaccines based on your puppy's risk factors.

After this, your puppy is done with vaccines for the year. However, you'll still need to make regular visits to the vet; the DHPP vaccine needs to be administered every year or two, and the rabies shot every one to three years. Make sure you stay on top of your dog's vaccinations; not only does it protect your dog's health, but it's also required by law in most locations.

Chapter 6: Puppies and Exercise

Much like humans, dogs need exercise to stay healthy both physically and mentally. Exercise keeps puppies fit, helps their bodies develop correctly, and provides a way for them to have fun while bonding with their owners.

However, you can't exactly buy your pup a gym membership, so you have to know a little more about how and when your dog should exercise.

A puppy is never too young to start exercising – especially if you've been going a little bit overboard with the treats in order to train him. The key to exercise with a young puppy is moderation. As we've mentioned previously, puppies can tire quickly, so you have to pay close attention to your pup and his needs. Never push your puppy too hard, and instead allow him to rest and rehydrate as often as needed.

To avoid overworking your puppy, exercise should initially be confined to brief but frequent periods throughout the week. You're better off to take your puppy on a five-minute walk twice a day than to wear him out with an hour-long walk once a week. Regular exercise, even for brief periods of time, will also be more beneficial for your puppy than trying to cram a week's worth of workouts into a single day.

You can alternate between the different methods of puppy exercise to keep things interesting as you build your puppy's endurance and wait for his body to develop. Maybe one day, the two of you go for a short walk; the next day, you might spend a little time splashing in the pool, or playing fetch in your backyard. There are plenty of ways to mix things up and make sure that exercise is fun and exciting for both you and your puppy.

Walking

Walking is perhaps the easiest and most common form of exercise for dogs. You can begin taking your puppy on walks as soon as he's leash-trained, and it's a great way for both you and your puppy to get out of the house, get some fresh air, and stretch those legs.

For young puppies, you need to be careful about the kind of surface you're walking on. Rough concrete, particularly when it's hot from the sun's rays, is tough on delicate little puppy paws. Instead, try to find an area to walk where the surface is gentler, such as through a grassy park. Once your puppy is older, his paws will be better able to withstand tough surfaces; however, you should always keep an eye on your dog and occasionally check his paws to make sure he doesn't have any injuries or damage.

Jogging

While jogging with your dog can be a great way for the both of you to get some exercise, you should never take a puppy jogging. The bodies of young puppies are still developing, and your pup's growing bones aren't yet able to withstand the impact of running. Instead, wait until your puppy is at least a year old before taking him jogging with you.

Playing

Playing is a great way to provide some exercise for pups of any age. Dig out your puppy's toy box and get creative. Play fetch or tug-of-war, and pretty soon both of you will forget that you're not only having fun, but also sneaking in some exercise!

Swimming

While some dogs enjoy swimming much more than others, this can be a great way for you and your puppy to have some fun and get some exercise. If your puppy dislikes water and seems fearful of swimming, certainly you should never force him in.

If your puppy does enjoy swimming, however, there are many things you can do to make the exercise extra fun. Pull some of you pup's (waterproof) toys in with you, and play fetch in the water.

However, always make sure that your puppy can't get in the water without your supervision. Prevent drowning accidents by keeping a close eye on your pup during playtime in the pool.

Exercise and Safety

Whenever you and your puppy head outside for some exercise, beware of the temperature. Dogs are more liable to overheat than humans, as dogs don't have any sort of sweat glands. Their only method of cooling down is panting, and while some panting is to be expected any time your puppy exercises or is outdoors in the heat, monitor him closely to avoid dehydration or heat exhaustion.

One of the easiest ways to prevent heat exhaustion is to limit the amount of time your puppy spends outside when it's hot. Take frequent breaks in shady areas, and bring along water to revitalize your puppy.

Never leave your dog alone in a car during the summer. Temperatures can climb quickly, and with no way of escaping, dogs may overheat and develop heat stroke, which might even lead to death.

Also, be especially careful with dog breeds that have respiratory issues. For example, dogs that have flat faces, such as pugs and bulldogs, often have difficulty breathing, which makes it challenging for them to regulate their temperature. As a result, these dogs have a very low heat tolerance, and so you need to be extra careful when exercising with them outdoors.

Even when you're being cautious and taking frequent breaks for rest in the shade and plenty of cool water, you should know and watch out for the signs of heat exhaustion in your puppy.

If you notice that your dog is panting excessively and having difficulty breathing, he may be developing heat exhaustion. Check to see if his tongue, the inside of his ears, and his nose are red; if so, panting isn't doing enough to regulate the temperature of his body. The puppy's saliva may become thick, and dogs with heat exhaustion often vomit and/or have diarrhea.

At this point, it is essential that you do anything you can to cool your puppy down. After heat exhaustion, a puppy may pass into heat stroke, which can result in death.

If your puppy demonstrates any of the signs of heat exhaustion, get him inside to an air-conditioned room as soon as possible, and make sure he has plenty of water. In the case of heat stroke, you may even need to place the puppy in a tub of cool water or situate him directly in front of a fan in order to cool him down.

Once your puppy seems to have recovered from an episode of heat exhaustion, take him to the veterinarian as soon as possible. The vet can ensure that no lasting damage was done.

However, with a bit of caution and consideration, you shouldn't ever have to worry about your puppy developing heat exhaustion. Simply allow frequent breaks and plenty of water, and nothing should stop you and your pup from having some fun in the sun!

Chapter 7: Loving Your Puppy

Many puppies love affection. They enjoy petting, cuddling, and curling up in the curve of your knee. They like to feel loved.

However, the biggest mistake pet owners can make when showing affection to their dog is treating it like a human being. While a pet may become like part of the family, it's important to remember that they are from a different species. Dogs think and feel differently than humans do, and they are highly driven by their instincts. Showing affection to a dog as you would to another human can be confusing or inappropriate, and it might even encourage negative behavior.

To start with, it's important to be mindful of *when* you show affection to your puppy. Many people will feel the urge to pet a frightened dog in order to comfort it, but this demonstration of affection only encourages fearful behavior. Instead, offer your puppy affection after he obeys your commands, exercises, or displays a calm and submissive attitude. Reward such positive behaviors with gentle petting and verbal praise.

When it comes to *how* you demonstrate affection to your dog, you should always be mindful of the fact that your pup's an animal and so has certain preferences about physical touch that differ from humans'. For example, many dogs don't like to be hugged. Pay attention to your puppy's physical cues as he reacts to any sort of physical touch, and if he seems uncomfortable, release him.

You should also avoid picking up your puppy once he gets a little older. Although it's natural for a mother to pick up her pup while he's very young, dogs are otherwise unaccustomed to being carried anywhere, and so the feeling can be disconcerting and they instinctively dislike it. Moreover, picking up a dog risks both injury, should he fall, and behavior problems, as it gives him the impression that he's bigger than he actually is and can cause him to become more aggressive.

Overall, the best way that you can show love to your puppy is by being a consistent, patient rule-giver who creates structure in the puppy's life. When you adopt a puppy, you become the "pack leader," so to speak, and the pup will look to you to provide direction and enforce rules. You don't want your puppy to think that *he's* the leader, as this will lead to all sorts of behavior problems such as disobedience and aggression. Instead, your puppy should be submissive to you and desire that you be a firm and strong leader.

By training your puppy to obey you, providing for his physical and mental needs, and enforcing the rules of the household, you establish yourself as the pack leader and demonstrate love for your puppy. In doing so, not only will you have an emotionally fulfilled pup, but you will also have a puppy that is well-behaved, obedient, and, overall, healthy and happy.

And when your puppy's happy, you will be too.

Conclusion

Thank you again for downloading *Puppy Training Guide: A Proven and Powerful Guide to Training Your Puppy in Obedience, Potty Training and Much More*!

I hope this book was able to help you learn how to train and care for your new puppy so that you can welcome him into your home and family.

The next step is to put what you've learned into action! That adorable, misbehaving ball of fur won't train itself, after all. Now it's time for you to get to work, and pretty soon, you'll have an obedient, well-behaved, and fully-trained puppy.

Finally, if you enjoyed this book, please take the time to share your thoughts and post a review on Amazon. It'd be greatly appreciated!

Thank you and good luck!

Blurb: So, you're thinking about getting a new puppy. You can't stop looking at pictures of pups and their little ears and their teeny tiny noses and their itty bitty paws. You can already envision yourself curling up with a sweet little puppy and welcoming him into your family. Are you only holding yourself back out of fear of what sort of destruction that adorable bundle of fur will wreak on your home, peace of mind, and relationships?

Fear no further!

Puppy Training Guide: A Proven and Powerful Guide to Training Your Puppy in Obedience, Potty Training and Much More tells you everything you could ever need to know about raising a puppy. We'll be with you every step of the way, from establishing rules for your puppy to training him to obey your commands. We'll even help you learn about caring for your puppy's health and happiness!

Adopting a puppy doesn't have to be a stressful situation when you know what you're doing. With *Puppy Training Guide*, you'll be expertly training your new puppy in no time!

www.ingramcontent.com/pod-product-compliance
Lightning Source LLC
Chambersburg PA
CBHW070258290526
45789CB00004B/1892